"I will proclaim the name of the Lord.
Oh, praise the greatness of our God!"
Deuteronomy 32:3

"An insightful book for those who have not experienced the challenges of cancer treatment. It gives encouragement to those who face or are going through treatment with the comfort and strength that comes while holding God's hand."

Rev. Conrad E. Lawrence, teacher
Henderson, NV

"Jill's book shares her story of surviving breast cancer, providing an example of a woman who is strengthened by her faith in Jesus Christ. The daily trials and challenges, that many will find familiar, are addressed with scripture offering support, direction, and comfort for the reader."

Katherine Hay, RN
Tuscaloosa, AL

"Cancer is an unfortunate reality in this broken world. Even so, cancer does not hold any ultimate power. In this reflection and devotional, Jill Simms walks the reader through her own spiritual journey through diagnosis and treatment, and then offers an incredibly rich daily resource for anyone dealing with the disease. Her faith in Christ is genuine and evident on every page. Her persistent hope through trials is inspiring. I could hear her voice as I read each page; this is no "put-on" spirituality. What she wrote is precisely how she talks. Conversational, engaging, and down to earth, Jill's testimony is a blessing."

Rev. Bob Davis,
Chula Vista, CA

"Jill's book, Sister to Sister, tells the story of her battle with breast cancer in an honest and detailed format that reveals the emotional anxiety and physical drain she faced. Yet through God's grace, her faith sustained her.

This is a story, not of instant healing, but of little miracles—an account coupled with pertinent devotionals that will encourage and strengthen anyone facing the enemy of cancer. Jill gives a compelling example of Christian growth through trails. Her book will help you believe that you too can go from victim to victor."

Rev. Brent Williams
Boulder City, NV

“If you have had to deal with the big “C” in your life or in a loved ones life, this book is a MUST READ. It can be anyone’s journey, but it brings you into a place of hope when you are probably feeling hopelessness. I lost my mom to breast cancer many years ago, and went on to work most of my life in the field of oncology. I wish I would have had this book to help get me through. Jill does a wonderful job of giving hope, and yes even JOY in the midst of a storm.”

Brenda Morrison
Greater Las Vegas Women’s Ministry

"To those who have been born again by God's Holy Spirit, Romans 8:28 teaches, "And we know that all things work together for good to them that love God, to them who are the called according to his purpose." He did not say that "all things" were pleasant nor easy. However, He did promise that we would go through them together with Him. (Psalm 23:4; John 6:37)

As we travel the rough road of life, we often find jewels upon the way. One of these on my rough road has been my sister, Jill. Although we were not blessed to know each other until our later years, I have found a sister who loves her family and friends and who has a deep abiding faith in her Lord. Through her ordeal with cancer, that faith has broadened and deepened.

Through her testimony, Jill holds out her hands to help others, with the needed empathy of one who has suffered in like manner. I pray that all who read her story will be driven to their knees to seek the help of the Great Physician, as she has."

John D. Stevenson Ph.D.
Author of "Restore Such A One, The Unpopular Command"

PRAISE GOD

Sister to Sister

A Survivors Guide

Jillene Simms

WestBow Press books may be ordered through booksellers or by contacting:

WestBow Press
A Division of Thomas Nelson & Zondervan
1663 Liberty Drive
Bloomington, IN 47403
www.westbowpress.com
1 (866) 928-1240

ISBN: 978-1-4908-5440-3 (sc)
ISBN: 978-1-4908-5441-0 (e)

Library of Congress Control Number: 2014918847

Printed in the United States of America.

WestBow Press rev. date: 12/12/2014

Dedicated to all who have had cancer touch their lives including patients, family members, friends, doctors, nurses, technicians, and those in research labs.

For you have been my hope, Sovereign Lord, my confidence since my youth. From birth I have relied on you; you brought me forth from my mother's womb, I will ever praise you.

—Psalm 71:5–6

Contents

Foreword

I have known this lady for quite some time. Besides being my wife, Jill has been my best friend for almost fifty-four years. I know her better than anyone on earth. I thought I knew her better than she knew herself, but then came the news of the lump. Wow! I learned more about her during the following year than I thought possible.

Jill is so much stronger, so much smarter, and so much more in touch with our Savior, Jesus Christ, than I am. She is comfortable with putting her troubles in His hands and trusting Him completely. I have always trusted in the Lord, but during this time I was having issues with Him and with our Father in heaven. My wife did more to help me deal with my faith problems than I did to help her through her troubles. Together, as always, we overcame our difficulties.

The journey took us from Jill's report of a lump through the first doctor's appointment, the biopsy, X-rays, CAT scans, the first and second surgeries, and on to the chemotherapy and the radiology treatments. On only one occasion, during her chemo treatment, did she refuse to listen to me or to the doctors. My wife can be bull-headed and she did not want to take the anti-nausea tablets until she needed them. Well, she learned to listen! That was the only time she had a problem. Jill did what people said was best for her. That's not to say she never questioned us, but when she did, her research, her prayer requests, and the answers she obtained always provided the correct path to travel.

Our difficult trek calls to mind the poem "Footprints in the Sand" by Margaret Fishback Powers. We walked along the beach with Jesus, and just as the poem says, when we looked down, we saw only one pair of footprints. They belonged to Jesus. He had carried us throughout our trip. Praise be to God, our Father in heaven.

—Grateful Husband and Best Friend, John C. Simms

Preface

All my life I have wanted to help people to know Jesus and His love for us. As I have gotten older and faced difficult situations, I have learned that God always works out our troubles for the best. This too has made me want to tell others about what a wonderful God we have. The same God who created heaven and earth cares about me and you.

Perhaps that is why God, placed this book on my heart. In August of 2013, while coming home from a checkup with my surgeon, I felt an impression upon my mind and my heart. The message was, "Write a book." *Lord, is that You?* I wondered. Then I felt the prompting again: "Write a book." I prayed and waited on God's timing and determined that this is what I should do.

During the following year I did my best to discern what God wanted me to do and to understand how He wanted me to do it. *Sister to Sister* is the result.

With the support of my husband, John, and my sons, John and Jeff, I have made it to this point. I also want to thank all my friends and family who have encouraged me to write.

Introduction

My story is not a tale of how God performed a huge miracle and cured me of cancer. It is a story of the many small miracles God performed to bless me. He sent me a deluxe bed, unexpected gifts, and the right doctors, to mention a few miracles. These things proved to me that God was in this fight with me. I wasn't alone. I know a lot of women have fought the same fight, and some had it a lot worse than I did. I don't want to make light of their experiences. I simply want to tell my story. Some women lost their fights, and my prayer is that at some point they asked Jesus into their hearts and are with Him now.

If God Can Heal …

I believe that God heals today. Sometimes He does a big miracle and instantly heals someone. There are testimonies from all over the world about that. So someone may ask, "Why didn't God just heal you?" Others will say, "If God really does heal today, why are there diseases to begin with and why do we need hospitals?" The simple truth is that we live in a fallen world and our bodies reflect that fact. Our bodies are affected by the way we treat them and by our environments. Some people don't ask God to heal them, and who knows what would happen if they did?

I did ask God to take away the lump in my breast and to protect me from cancer. I prayed alone and I had people pray with me. Then I waited to see what would happen. I was in North Carolina when I discovered my lump. I would lie in bed at night looking out the window, wondering what the future would bring. I was focused on getting my husband and me out of North Carolina before winter hit. I prayed and prayed. The sense I got was to go ahead and move and that things would turn out fine. I just needed to trust that God would oversee my situation and take care of me and my family. This was not the first time I had faced a serious health problem, but it was the biggest challenge to my faith. Through prayer and Scripture reading I remained upright in my faith. I hope that what I learned will help others fighting cancer.

Chapter 1

I Have a Lump

Do not withhold your mercy from me, O Lord;
may your love and your truth always protect me.

—Psalm 40:11

I have a lump. I have a lump. I was practicing the words in my head as I walked into the garage. I couldn't put it off any longer. I had to tell my husband and son that I had a lump in my breast. John, my husband, and Jeff, my son, were in the garage unpacking boxes. We had just moved into our new home in Nevada. It was a hot July day, and they were sitting on stools resting. Sweat ran down their faces as they looked up to acknowledge me.

"This is hard, but I need to tell you something," I said. John looked straight at me, and his body stiffened as if he were bracing himself. We had been together fifty years, since high school, and he knew me well. I'm sure he could tell by my voice something wasn't right. Jeff looked down to the floor, but I knew he was listening. Sharing the news was difficult, and I started to cry with the first words. "I have a lump," I told them. "I have had it for a while, and I will be going to the doctor tomorrow to have it looked at."

John's face turned white as he took a deep breath. Because John is a retired pharmacist, I'm sure all the medical considerations were going through his head, and of course he was concerned for my well-being. John didn't speak, and Jeff said little. I think they were in shock. I seemed to have thrown ice-cold water on both of them.

This was probably the first time I had faced the fact that I might have cancer. I had kept the lump a secret for several months. I don't remember when I first noticed it. I found the lump doing a self-exam in the shower while we were still in North Carolina. Sometimes it was there and sometimes it wasn't. I had had lumps in the past, and they had never been a problem. The doctor would drain them, and they would always be benign. I was not worried about the possibility of cancer. Since our move, the area around the lump had begun to hurt and to swell a little. So it was time to get the lump examined. It was not going away.

Though we had been in Nevada for only six months, in some ways it felt as if we had been there for years. John and I moved to Henderson, Nevada, from Black Mountain, North Carolina, in December 2010. We wanted to escape North Carolina before the snow hit, and we just made it. The first snow came the day we left. To make our move, we rented an RV from North Carolina to Nevada. John's health had been declining for several years as a result of neck surgeries that left him with peripheral neuropathy. He was in major pain twenty-four hours a day. The RV made sense. Besides, we didn't want to put our black Lab, Lady Bug, on a plane.

Our son John and his wife Claudia saved up vacation time to help us make the cross-country drive. This was sort of a working vacation for them. We enjoyed being together after living apart for six years. John was able to stretch his six-foot-four body out on the bed from time to time, relieving his pain.

About a week after leaving North Carolina, we were in a rented house. John and Claudia returned home to California. After all, it was almost Christmas!

Jeff and his black Lab, Jewel, had come from California to visit for Christmas. Jeff was thinking of moving in with us, so we were eager to find out if the dogs would get along. A few days after Christmas the doorbell rang. Both dogs ran full speed, their feet sliding on the tile floor, to the front door, getting there before I did. Through the window beside the door I could see a woman with beautiful white hair holding a plate of cookies. "Jeff," I called, "can you help?" He grabbed the dogs by their collars, and I finally got the door open. "Hi," I said. With a big smile on her face, the woman answered, "I'm Janet Lawrence. My husband, Conrad, and I live across the street. I know Christmas has passed, but here are some Christmas cookies for you." Janet's kindness started a friendship that gets better and better as the years pass. This was one of the miracles that we received after moving to Nevada.

We got the keys to our own home on Mother's Day in May 2011 and were completely moved by the first of June. Jeff and Jewel had moved in with us, and by the time my birthday arrived in July, we were almost finished unpacking. We were settled in enough to invite our granddaughters, Valeria, fifteen, and Andrea, fourteen, to visit us for a week. They were on hand along with our son John for my sixty-fifth birthday. My husband and our sons got together and decided that I needed a television for my bedroom as a gift. We had no idea how handy the television would be in the next year.

So there we were in our new home, in a new city and a new state with new doctors, facing something that we never thought we would face.

Chapter 2

Meet Dr. El-Eid

> Do not be anxious about anything, but in everything, by prayer and petition, with thanksgiving, present your requests to God. And the peace of God, which transcends all understanding, will guard your hearts and your minds in Christ Jesus.
>
> —Philippians 4:6–7

I took a deep breath and opened the door. Was I scared? Yes, I was! Seeing a new doctor is always difficult let alone one who deals with cancer. In the waiting room I saw a sign on the wall that read, "I pray for your safekeeping. Be encouraged." A doctor in Las Vegas, Nevada, who prays! I knew God had put me in the right place. I thought about how I got there. The doctor whom John and I usually see was on vacation, so I scheduled an appointment with his associate. This physician had met Dr. Souzan El-Eid at a teaching event and gave me a referral. I later learned that if I had seen our regular doctor he would have sent me to someone else because he didn't know of Dr. El-Eid. There are many wonderful doctors out there, but the Lord knew my personality, my strengths, and my weaknesses. He also knew why I should have this doctor.

"But be assured today that the Lord your God is the one who goes across ahead of you like a devouring fire" (Deuteronomy 9:3).

I did the usual filling out of forms and we waited. John and Jeff had come with me for support. We were all pretty tense. The nurse soon called my name. In the exam room the nurse took my blood pressure and my temperature and asked me to put on a paper blouse. This wasn't a full gown, just the top half, which was something new for me. The only good thing I can say about it is that it was pink.

The door opened slowly and the doctor entered and read my name. I answered yes, wishing I wasn't there. Dr. El-Eid looked up at me, walking and reading my chart at the same time. My first impression of her was her long, curly hair. For a small person, she had a lot of hair. It was nicely pulled back on one side to reveal her smile as she greeted me. As she walked closer, I noticed toenails peeking out from her sandals. Her polish was a bright, almost neon pink. *What a fun thing*, I thought. *This woman truly likes the color pink.* Of course she would—that is the color for breast cancer awarness.

She continued to read my chart and exclaimed, "Why are you taking hormones? Don't you know they cause breast cancer?" I thought to myself, *Oops! Not a good start.* Strike one. I explained why I was on them and said I had been a little afraid to stop taking them. *Whew,* I thought. *That was hard.* She asked when I had had my last mammogram. I had to admit I had not had one since we moved to North Carolina six years before. Oops again. Strike two. When we lived in California I got mammograms yearly, and they always came out just fine. For some reason I never got another after we moved. One time I made an appointment but had to cancel because of work and never rescheduled.

The next big question from the doctor was, "Why didn't you come in sooner with this lump?" Oops again. Strike three. The question was difficult. I seemed to have done everything wrong. The truth is that I had been overwhelmed with life for the last year and a half. My parents had passed away within six months of each other, and I was the executor of the estate. John's health was slipping, and we needed to get out of North Carolina before winter. Dr. El-Eid looked up at me and smiled. "You know when I was younger I would have really been upset," she said, "but now I understand that sometimes these things happen." I breathed a sigh of relief. I wanted to finish the tests. The doctor helped me forget the past and not whip myself over decisions that were made or not made. We needed to take care of the task at hand.

Because the doctor had her own ultrasound machine, she could do the test in her office right away. That was a blessing, since I didn't have to wait for another appointment in a different office. During the ultrasound, she showed me on the screen the area that concerned her. Time was short that day, so I needed to return in a few days for the biopsies.

The day of the biopsy I did all the little tricks that I do to lift myself up. My hair looked good. I polished my nails to match my red outfit and wore a favorite necklace, one that I save for special occasions. Jeff and John went with me for moral support. I asked John to join me in the exam room because I was scared, not knowing what would take place. Fear of the unknown is monumental for me. Normally I can keep it under control and have faith that all will be okay. On this occasion my fear of the unknown was coupled with fear of pain. I took things one small step at a time to get through the day. Fear had taken over, and I didn't feel at peace with the Lord.

The doctor explained everything that would happen, but hearing about the biopsy and undergoing it were two different things. Dr. El-Eid would perform the procedure with the help of a nurse. She would do a needle biopsy into the lymph node area, followed by a biopsy on the lump area. The doctor promised that after a local injection the needle wouldn't hurt, and she was right. The experience was similar to going to the dentist. After that first shot, I could relax a little.

With the ultrasound machine guiding the needles, we started. When Dr. El-Eid began to drill, I panicked, but John was at my side, holding my hand and telling me to look into his eyes, and that helped me get through the procedure. Our fear can be compounded when we hear what is happening but can't see it. However, I didn't want to see what was going on. When it was over, the doctor told me I had been brave. I think she was being nice because she knew I had panicked. Then again, perhaps you are brave when you carry on in the face of your fears.

When we got home from the doctor's office, all I wanted to do was get into something comfortable and take a nap. To my surprise, I also wanted to hold my cat, Shelby. She had been my love muffin. She was eighteen pounds, soft and fluffy, and great to snuggle with. The only problem was that Shelby had died more than a year before at the advanced age of sixteen. I felt sad all over again at the thought of her passing.

The next day I asked Janet to take me to a store. I was hurting and didn't want to drive. I found a toy cat that looked almost exactly like Shelby. It was white and had blue eyes like hers. The toy was battery-operated and purred when you petted it. This was a silly indulgence, but it was one of the things I did to get through my adventure. When I returned home from shopping I went straight to my room. The rustling of the shopping bag drew both the dogs into my room to investigate. I took the cat from the box and turned it on. When the cat moved, Lady Bug took immediate notice. She and Shelby had been pals. Lady Bug checked out the cat from one end to the other and finally decided it wasn't Shelby. Still, she laid her nose on the toy cat and nuzzled it. I thank God for the blessings and miracles that come to us through our pets.

We had to wait a few days for the biopsy results. The doctor's office was fifty minutes from our home, so I gave her permission to phone the results to me when she got them. We would make plans from there. A few days later she called. I picked up the phone in my bedroom. She asked if I was ready for the results. I said yes. I sat on the end of the bed to support myself. Dr. El-Eid told me I had cancer. I felt a little bit of relief that at least we knew what we were dealing with. The doctor said that it was stage one, which was a very good thing. She also said that the cancer was caused by hormones. Now came the hard part—telling my family.

Chapter 3

Surgery

The earliest date Dr. El-Eid could get me in for surgery was about ten days away. It would be on August 10. The ten days we had to wait went by quickly. There were blood tests to be run and arrangements to be made. John and I had discussed lumpectomy versus mastectomy with the doctor, but I had not made a decision yet. A mastectomy seemed radical for my diagnosis, but the doctor explained that it was an easier surgery from her standpoint.

I know women who have had mastectomies just because they wanted to get rid of all the breast tissue, removing any chance of reoccurrence. With the reconstructive surgery available now, a mastectomy is a quick choice for some and a necessary choice for others. I found it hard to think about. At first I liked the idea of getting rid of all the tissue, but then the idea began to bother me. The decision was not as easy as it seemed. Would the surgery affect my husband? I didn't want to have a mastectomy if it was not necessary. I needed to seek God's wisdom. He knows what is best for me and He knows my future.

John and I discussed the possibilities, but he left the decision up to me, which I appreciated. He didn't pressure me either way. I continued to pray about it, but I was baffled because I wasn't getting any direction from the Lord. I remained undecided until I was sitting on the exam table, waiting for the doctor to make final arrangements. As she was asking which choice we had made, I heard "That one" and felt a tremendous peace about it. It would be a lumpectomy. Waiting on instructions from the Lord can be hard, but when He speaks, you know His voice.

I like to plan things out. I want to know what will happen, when it will happen, and how it will happen. Learning to wait on the Lord has been hard for me. When I am tempted to jump in and make my own plans, knowing full well I was told to wait, I stop myself and recall Abraham and Sara and how long they waited to hear from God. (Read Genesis chapters 15, 16, and 21.) They interfered with God's plan when they got tired of waiting, lost faith in His promise, and created their own plan. So, over the years, I have learned to wait and listen. When I finally hear, I recognize God's leading because I feel that great peace that comes with knowing. I am sure it is God's peace because it comes from my innermost being. The feeling is not just emotional but mental and physical. I seem to be glowing from the center of my torso. My breathing slows down and my muscles relax. I realize that I don't need all the answers as to what is going on. The stress is gone.

"The man who enters by the gate is the shepherd of his sheep. The watchman opens the gate for him, and the sheep listen to his voice. He calls his own sheep by name and leads them out. When he has brought out all his own, he goes on ahead of them, and his sheep follow him because they know his voice" (John 10:2–4).

I had never had an outpatient surgery and wasn't sure what to expect. I have learned through experience that no surgery should be taken for granted. Surgery is surgery, and there is always a chance that the unexpected will happen. You do the best you can in choosing a doctor and a facility and you pray, but at some point you must leave the rest in God's hands.

I had sent out prayer requests across the United States, so I knew I was well covered spiritually. Nonetheless I asked John; Jeff; our pastor, Brent Williams; Janet, and Conrad to pray with me a few days before surgery. They laid hands on me in prayer and I was anointed with oil. Our prayer time was filled with the Holy Spirit, and I had a great sense of peace about the surgery to come. Right before the operation, a friend called and said that the Lord had shown her angels lining the halls of the hospital. What a God I have! He cares so much about me that He sent His angels to help me.

The surgery day came, and we had to get up early to reach the hospital by six in the morning. It was an hour's drive, and we had not been there before. When John and I were waiting in the surgery prep area, we told the nurses it was our fiftieth anniversary of going steady and asked if they thought we should get married. They all laughed. August 10, 1961, was the day that John asked me to go steady with him. Thinking about that day was emotional for us. We were two scrawny teenagers and had gone to the beach on a Sunday afternoon. Remembering that day helped distract us from the serious business ahead. We were eager to get the surgery over with and hear that the cancer had been removed.

One by one the nurses did their part to get me ready. Then the anesthesiologist introduced herself to me. When Dr. El-Eid appeared she looked different in her scrubs, but her great smile remained. She was just as eager to finish the process as we were. The time came and both doctors and a nurse wheeled me to the surgery room. Cancer surgeons often have a pathologist in the operating room with them. As the surgeon removes pieces of the diseased area, the spot is checked under a microscope to determine whether more tissue must be taken out. The reading must be accurate to guide surgeons in their decisions.

Dr. El-Eid had told us that she would cut a wide margin, offering the best chance of getting all the cancer cells. Although the surgery pathologist may think the samples are cancer free, doctors don't know until they do more tests in the lab. Only then can they be sure that the cancer is entirely removed.

As far as I was concerned, the surgery went quickly. The anesthesiologist did a good job. She said, "Okay, tell me if you feel a little light-headed." I said, "I feel it," and she said, "Now I will give you more of an injection. Just count backwards, starting at a hundred." I think I might of said, "Ninety-nine, ninety-eight, ninety-seven." Next thing I knew she was waking me up, saying the surgery was over. I remember being moved to the recovery area. I could hear the voices of nurses and other patients.

After an hour or so, attendants woke me again and offered me juice. They brought my clothes and asked me to change in the bathroom. I had brought a lightweight duster and slippers. This attire would make it easier to climb into bed when I got home. All I wanted to do was sleep, but not a chance. I managed to get into my duster and into a wheelchair.

A few minutes later attendants were pushing me out the door, and there was my husband, John, with a huge smile on his face. I could see the relief that he felt as I appeared. Our sons, Jeff and John, had gone to get the car, and so off we went. They had brought a pillow and a blanket for me to use on the ride home. I slept the whole way. Our son John had come up from California for the day to be with us. It was nice having him there. The guys helped me into the house and into bed. Lady Bug and Jewel knew something wasn't quite right with Mom and didn't do their usual jumping around, but they came to my bedside to check me out.

It felt so good to be in my bed. I was grateful that the surgery was over. I thanked God for the blessings of a family close by and went to sleep. At about 7 p.m. I woke to the wonderful smell of hamburgers cooking. I hadn't eaten since the day before. Did I dare eat one? Yes, of course, and it sure tasted great! Better yet, it stayed down. The next morning I couldn't believe how good I felt. I was sore but able to get up and go to the family room and enjoy time with the guys.

A few days later we went to Dr. El-Eid's office to have her check me out. Our hearts were light as we drove to my appointment. John and I went into the exam room and waited. Dr. El-Eid came in but she wasn't happy. The tests had come back from the lab. There was more cancer, and I would need another surgery. The doctor was upset because she had never had to do two surgeries on the same patient. John and I were stunned and almost speechless. We listened closely as she gave us all the details. We asked questions and then I said something like, "Well, when can we do the next surgery and get this stuff out of me?" Dr. El-Eid was pleased that I wanted to get it over with quickly.

The surgery was August 23. Everything was pretty much the same except I had a different pathologist. The nurses did a double take on hearing my name, and this was somewhat amusing. "Weren't you just in here?" they asked. I explained and they said how unusual it was for my doctor to need to go in twice. Dr. El-Eid was still upset about doing the relumpectomy, and she sat with John and me as we waited in the prep area.

This operation was different. It was more aggressive, and some of my lymph nodes were removed, which required two incisions. I went home with a drain bag. I didn't wake up bright and cheery and didn't want any dinner this time. I felt as if an eighteen-wheeler had hit me. Dr. El-Eid said this was because I had undergone anesthesia twice in a relatively short time.

As usual my husband, John, and son Jeff were at my side taking care of me. As my drain tube filled up the little pouch, it had to be emptied and a drainage measurement taken. John would make careful calculations and write them down, noting the time of day the tube was emptied. Thanks to prayer and tender loving care, when I saw the doctor she was able to remove my tube and the real healing could begin. She gave me simple exercises to do to keep my surgery area from getting stiff and causing loss of movement in my shoulder and my arm.

Now I could move on to the following phase of treatment. Dr. El-Eid had helped me pick out my next doctors. The cancer center had locations all over the valley, and the doctors she recommended were closer to my home. That was a blessing for us because there would be many more appointments to come.

Chapter 4
The Quilt

I was blessed that John was able to accompany me to most of my appointments. I think the doctors liked having him there too. Having a second set of ears is always a good idea because there are so many instructions to remember. We were meeting a new doctor. Dr. Khoi M. Dao had a friendly way about him and was easy to talk to. As we got acquainted, we discovered that the medical school he attended was one that my father had helped to build in 1965 in Southern California. I could hardly believe it. I saw this as another small miracle that God performed to show that He was in this adventure with me.

The cancer center provided patients with binders of information. The center at which I was a patient was conducting cancer studies, and the staff asked if I would like to participate. The study was divided into three sections. The center would draw a paper from a container to determine your group assignment. Patients in two of the sections would take combinations of current medications and experimental medications. There was a chance that this treatment would not work. If I wound up in one of these groups and the medications failed, I would need further treatments until the cancer was gone.

I was given time to think about the proposal and papers to read to help me decide. I wanted to help the fight against cancer. Studies like this are one of the reasons medical science has come such a long way in treating the disease. After much reading and prayer, I said yes to the study. I felt a peace from God, signaling that I should go ahead with it. I felt that God would be in charge and that I would end up in the leg of the study that was best for me.

This decision meant more papers to sign. I was assigned a nurse who would watch me closely and be with me during most of my chemo treatments. I ended up in the group undergoing the current cancer treatment. Thank You, Jesus. This meant that I would be helping the research and getting the best care available. I learned later that some of the patients receiving the experimental treatments had terrible reactions to the medications and were forced to drop out. I prayed for them and asked God to bless them for their courage and willingness to help cancer research. When you are in a trial, you become a number and all your records are closely guarded.

"Be strong and courageous. Do not be afraid or terrified because of them, for the Lord your God goes with you; he will never leave you nor forsake you" (Deuteronomy 31:6).

My doctor had suggested that I have a port inserted into my chest for the chemo treatments. Not all patients get ports and some can't for medical reasons.

Having the port put in was a simple procedure that took about an hour. The operation required some courage on my part. Although the target area was numb, I was awake during the procedure as I had been for my biopsies. During the biopsies, the doctor poked or drilled holes with special equipment. This time, however, the doctor would be using a scalpel and making two incisions. Maybe this seemed easy since I had gone through two biopsies and two surgeries. I had more peace about me. I was not overcome by fear as I had been with the biopsies.

As usual there was a lot of prayer before the procedure. Because this was a sterile room, I couldn't have John at my side this time. A nurse was assigned to stand beside me. He watched the monitors and made conversation, helping to keep my mind off of what was happening. We talked about the passing of Michael Jackson and about the drugs that he had been using. Except for one female nurse who came and went, the doctor and the nurses were all guys. This felt weird, but I sensed that I was safe. They asked if there was anything they could do for me, and I said that I wanted a teddy bear to hold. "Oh!" someone said, laughing. "That would be Jim [not his real name]. That is why he is standing next to you." I replied, "All right. How about a cup of coffee?" Jim promised that he would get me one when the procedure was over. He brought me fresh-brewed coffee in the recovery room.

The Lord gave me the courage I needed. I kept telling myself that having courage doesn't mean you don't have fear. It means that you can move ahead regardless of the fear. In my mind I returned to this Scripture verse time and time again:

"He will cover you with his feathers, and under his wings you will find refuge; his faithfulness will be your shield and rampart" (Psalm 91:4).

I started my chemo treatments a couple of days later. The first treatment took five hours or more. That morning I packed up my things in a beautiful bag that had been made for me. This was another of the miracles that helped me get through my adventure.

My sister-in-law, Linda, loves to make lap quilts. I was unaware that she had started one for me. She had planned on giving it to me for my birthday and had used the colors of my bedroom—pink, lavender, white, and a pale yellow—in the quilt. On the day that I was diagnosed with cancer, a box arrived at the house. I opened it and to my surprise found not only a beautiful quilt but also a matching tote bag in which to carry it.

This gift became my chemo quilt, and when I was under it I felt safe and covered with the Lord's protection. The center kept the chemo room at a low temperature to reduce the chance of bacterial infection. Chemo patients have weakened immune systems and need to guard against infections of all kinds. The chemo nurses were good about giving patients blankets, but I felt that my quilt was God-given through Linda and that I had a part of her with me. I used the bag to carry not just the quilt but my iPod and cell phone, little hard candies to suck on, a book, and whatever else I thought I would need during my eighteen weeks of treatments.

Jeff and John drove me to treatments. They would wait until I was taken back to the room and would return a few hours later when the treatment was over. During my first treatment, however, John sat nearby, making sure that I didn't have a bad reaction to the chemo. After that session, we went out to dinner to celebrate the beginning of the end of my treatments. We wanted to have a good memory to go with them. Since the doctor had given me lots of medication to keep me from throwing up, I felt quite well.

The next day Jeff drove me to the doctor's office for an injection, which I would get each time I had a chemo treatment. The medication was Neulasta, a white-blood-cell booster. The doctor had explained to me that through the years Neulasta was found to work a lot better if patients got it the day after treatment. I still wasn't feeling too bad. My energy level was low, and I felt a little light-headed. I had no reaction to the shot beyond fatigue. Dr. Dao had given me two prescriptions to keep me from throwing up. He told me that I probably would not feel the side effects of the chemo treatment for a day or two.

I can't remember what time of day it was, but John stopped by my room and asked, "Would you like anything for nausea?" I felt good and said, "No. I don't think I need it yet." Five minutes later I was running to the bathroom to throw up. John helped get me back into bed. He brought one of my pills and placed a bucket beside the bed. John said he could tell by the look on my face that I was going to throw up. I guess I should have taken the pill when he first asked. Lesson one: take a pill before you think you need it. I praise God for this medication because that was the only time I threw up while I was being treated.

The next two days were a blur. I just slept. I would get up to go to the bathroom and even make it into the shower but then go right back to bed. By the third day I felt well enough to sit in the family room and watch TV. Chemo can give you muscle cramps, and I got them in my legs. One of my favorite things in the whole world is having my feet rubbed, and John would rub my legs and my feet at night. I know that he was sometimes tired, but he would do it anyway.

About seven days after treatment I felt okay, and that feeling lasted about a week. I didn't want to leave the house unless I had to go to the doctor, but I felt well enough to knit or to watch a movie without falling asleep. After the third week of treatment I had some energy and could usually make it to church or take a quick trip to a store. Then at the end of the week I faced another treatment, and the cycle would start all over again.

I had six treatments, one every three weeks. Sometimes I would take reading or knitting to do during the chemo session. As I got closer to the end of the treatments, I would tire quickly and would want to nap. During chemo, your brain doesn't quite work right. Some people call it chemo fog. Whatever you call this side effect, it makes it hard to concentrate on what you are doing or to remember what you did.

I noticed little interaction between the patients—probably because everyone was napping. This was in part because the meds that kept you from throwing up made you sleepy. I almost never sat next to the same person, but I remember one young woman. She was in her late twenties or early thirties. Her cancer was blood-related. We chatted for a few minutes and then she excused herself so she could nap. She told me that she had three children under age five, including twins, and that her chemo session gave her time to sleep. *Oh Lord*, I thought, *I am so grateful that I don't have small children to take care of during this time.*

The chemo room was bright with sunlight. Men and women sat in recliners, with the nurses keeping a close watch on everyone. The nurses had loving ways of working with us. Every once in a while they would come by with a basket of individually wrapped crackers and cookies and offer them to us. They also brought us juice or water if we wanted it. Having a little something in your stomach helped. I often thought that the nurses had a special calling for this work because they were so caring and sincere.

Seeing male patients reminded me that there are many kinds of cancer. Some people were getting blood transfusions to correct the damage done by the chemo to their blood. Chemo causes your red-blood-cell count to drop—thus the need for transfusions. I was blessed that my counts stayed good and didn't decrease much until my last treatment. I attribute this to prayer, good doctors, and the grace of our Lord.

The last chemo treatment was difficult for some reason. The nurse had problems getting the port hooked up. I was tense, which didn't help the nurse. It took three nurses to finally get the port connected, and by that time I was in tears. When the treatment was finished, I was ecstatic to be out of there. When I got home I found a beautiful bouquet of roses from John waiting for me to celebrate my last treatment. I was immensely relieved that I would not need to return to the chemo room.

Chapter 5

Buzz Cut

> Are not two sparrows sold for a penny? Yet not one of them will fall to the ground apart from the will of your Father. And even the very hairs of your head are all numbered. So don't be afraid; you are worth more than many sparrows.
>
> —Matthew 10:29–31

For a long time I had wondered what I would look like bald, but I never thought I would find out. My curiosity started many years before with a sci-fi movie that included a young woman without hair. In an interview, the actress said that she had shaved her head and showed up for the audition bald. She made quite an impression on me. I thought she was striking. Of course in the movie she wore lots of makeup, but she looked good.

My surgeon had given me several good resource books. Among the information brochures was a booklet listing the shops in our area that sold wigs. The booklet also explained how to get a wig if you didn't have the money to buy one. Several organizations help cancer patients get things they need. I looked up the wig shops listed in the book on the Internet. This was a great strategy since I didn't feel like driving all over.

I was still sore from my surgeries and still stressed, so this was not a good time to be driving. With the help of the websites, I narrowed my search to a couple of stores. Janet offered to drive me to check them out, and I jumped at the suggestion.

The first place we visited was wonderful. The shop specialized in helping chemo patients and was close to the doctors I would be seeing for chemo and radiation. The woman who owned the shop was a licensed cosmetologist and helped in several ways. The shop carried not only wigs but special soaps and lotions. During chemo and radiation your skin can become quite damaged. When we finished checking out the shop, Janet and I went out to her car. We talked and prayed about the experience and decided that we didn't need to visit the other place. This one was wonderful and its prices were competitive. I also liked the fact that the shop contributed to organizations fighting breast cancer.

The next week I had an appointment to choose a wig and order it. I wanted John and Jeff to go with me. They gladly accompanied me to a place a guy would not normally visit. I was leaning toward a wig about the same color as my hair, but for fun I tried on a blond wig. I wish I had taken a picture of John's face! He decided right away that I looked much better with dark auburn hair. Making a choice was hard, so I did what every good shopper does: I bought more than one. I ended up with three! I know this was extravagant, but sometimes you need to break with life's normal pattern to get through your trials.

My favorite wig was short and weighed only an ounce and a half. It was so light I hardly knew I had it on. The other two were a little longer and of different styles. The varied types worked well. I needed a wig for about eleven months. The heavier ones were handy during the winter, and the light one was great on hot days or when I was in the house. I would periodically have to wash and style a wig, so I needed another to wear in the meantime.

The wigs made now are stylish and lightweight. In the 1970s wigs were in vogue and I had one then. I liked putting on a new look without the fuss of doing my hair. There is no comparison between the wigs back then and the ones sold now. They have improved greatly. I have had curly hair all my life, so one of the fun parts of a wig was that my hair would be straight and in a cute style that I didn't have to fix every day.

There are many types of head coverings and many resources to help you get just the right one for your head. I never realized how cold my head would get without hair. Our heavenly Father gives us a natural head covering, just another way He takes care of us. I purchased two sleep caps because even the pillow case felt cold. I already had a drawer full of scarves. A hat also proved handy. The wind will blow right through your wig, and you'll be even colder if it rains. A hat helps keep your wig on in the wind. Depending on the hat, you may not need to wear a wig at all.

I had been told that your hair starts to fall out about fifteen days after your first chemo treatment. I made an appointment at the shop for the fourteenth day after my first session to have the owner shave my head. I had been told by other survivors that it was better to cut off my hair and not wait for it to fall out on its own. It would come out in the shower, they said, and I would find it on my sheets in the morning. I also learned that my head would be tender when the hair started to fall out. A few days before my appointment, my head did in fact become tender. I was glad when the day of my appointment arrived because my head was sore and my hair was definitely falling out.

Janet drove me to the appointment and sat close by during the process. Just for fun, we took a couple of pictures with my cell phone. The shop owner was ready to do the buzzing. She was sweet and considerate. She swung my chair away from the mirror as she turned on the clippers, sparing me the sight of my hair falling to the ground. I had not thought about the trauma of watching this happen. Her kindness again proved that God had led me to the right place. I brought a baggie to store the cuttings so I could give them to John. He loves my curly hair and would miss seeing it. Putting my hair in a bag was a bit of a joke to help keep things light. Then the shop owner helped me put on my new wig. When we left the shop, Janet and I went out to lunch. This was fun because I knew that a little secret was hidden under the wig.

I had told only relatives what I was doing that day and asked them to pray. That night, however, I got an e-mail from a friend in North Carolina. She said that God had asked her to keep me covered in prayer that day. What a wonderful heavenly Father I have. He knew how much prayer I needed. My friend had no idea what was going on, but she was obedient and prayed. The victory goes to the Lord. I saw in this another miracle that got me through my adventure.

This short straight wig was my favorite. I would get many compliments on my hair style. I would just smile and say "thank you."

Chapter 6

The Bed

> If you, then, though you are evil, know how to give good gifts to your children, how much more will your Father in heaven give good gifts to those who ask him!
>
> —Matthew 7:11

During chemo and radiation treatments you get tired. I never would have guessed how much of a blessing a bed could be. My heavenly Father knew how much, though, and performed another miracle for me.

In 2007 when John and I were living in North Carolina, I was shopping for a bed that would rise at the head and the feet. John had a lot of leg pain because of his illness and had fallen and broken both ankles. I thought that such a bed would relieve his pain at night. I had shopped at a few furniture places, but I wasn't sure where to find the bed I wanted.

One day I decided to phone a friend and ask if she knew where to shop. She was not someone I shopped with and we weren't especially close, but I kept thinking I should call her. I finally did, but she didn't know of a store that might help. Then she asked, "Would you object to a slightly used bed?

You could consider it as God's provision for us." She explained that her mother was moving into a care facility and needed to downsize. My friend would be visiting her mother's home in St. Louis in a few weeks to help her make the transition and would be returning with furniture in a rental truck. Her mother had just what I was looking for in her guest bedroom. Did I want it? She wasn't sure if her mother would give up the bed. Still, I could hardly wait to answer, "Yes. What a blessing it would be!" The little shopping I had done showed me how expensive those beds could be.

I didn't know when my friend left on her trip, and I almost forgot about the bed. I was just waiting to hear from her. Then one Sunday I went forward in church for prayer. The woman who prayed for me got a vision of a truckload of gifts coming my way. She said that God was blessing me with many gifts. Wow! How wonderful was that! It never dawned on me that the bed might be one of those gifts until the next day when my friend phoned and said she was on her way back and had the bed for us! Her mother had decided that morning to give it to us.

They took a few days to arrive. As I was painting the master bedroom to get it ready for the new bed, questions swirled in my mind. What did the bed look like? Would it fit? Could we get it into the room with the tight corners in the hall? Would my spread fit? I was beset by details. I had to give myself a little talking-to and remind myself that if God was bringing a bed to us from that far away, He knew that it would fit!

The truck arrived late in the day, and the bed was beyond belief. It didn't simply move up and down; it had a massage unit. And my friend's mother had also given us the spread with matching pillow shams, blanket, mattress pads, and four sets of sheets. Some of the sheets were still in the packages! These were the types of things that I would have picked out myself. They were perfect for me! So the woman with the vision was right. There was a truck with lots of gifts from the Lord! The curious thing is that because of John's special circumstances, he has never been able to use the bed, so it became mine. This was one of the ways God helped me get through my bout with cancer. I felt blessed every time I got into His special gift.

"I will lie down and sleep in peace, for you alone, O Lord, make me dwell in safety" (Psalm 4:8).

Chapter 7

Glowing in the Dark

> Be joyful always; pray continually; give thanks in all circumstances, for this is God's will for you in Christ Jesus.
>
> —1 Thessalonians 5:16–18

The chemo treatments ended, and I had an appointment with my radiation doctor the following week. God certainly seemed to have selected the group of doctors who treated me. As it turned out, Dr. Matthew Schwartz, the radiation doctor, grew up in the same town I had. We were from different generations, but we remembered the same things about the place. He was about the age of my sons but had attended a different school than they did. I didn't begin to feel that I was getting older until my doctors started to be the same age as my sons. Now the doctors' staff members are about the age of my granddaughters! Well almost.

Dr. Schwartz wanted to start my radiation right away, but I needed a little time to rest from chemo and get my port removed. He was nice about it and scheduled me to start in three weeks. I knew why the doctor wanted to start immediately, but the port was irritating my chest and I badly wanted to have it out. The downside of taking time off from care is that you start to get out of the treatment mode and don't want to return.

Before you start treatments, location readings must be done for the radiation machine. You need to lie perfectly still as a camera passes back and forth over your body. Technicians find the exact spots where they will line up the radiation machine. Once they identify these spots with a felt-tip marker, they replace the ink marks with little tattoos. I felt like asking the technician why he didn't give me something cute like a heart or butterflies instead of four boring black dots, but he was concentrating on his work, so I tried not to disturb him too much. When my sons found out I had tattoos, they started calling me their "tattooed mom."

While I was on the table, my wig came off. I'm not sure why. Maybe it was just because I was lying down. I had to ask the technician to retrieve it from the table for me. I was laughing, probably out of embarrassment, and he was pretending that he didn't notice. You need to find humor when and where you can. I felt blessed that the technician was extremely polite and respectful of my feelings.

I imagine that each doctor's office runs a little differently, but the way mine was set up suited me just fine. We were given cubbyholes with our names on them. At the beginning of the week we would get fresh gowns. After each treatment we would put the gowns in the cubbyholes for the next day. I found it interesting to see the different ways patients stored the gowns. Some were folded neatly, some were wadded up and stuck in, and some hung out over the shelves. We had different types of cancer and different personalities to help us deal with the stress. This was another reminder that cancer can happen to anyone and that it is a great equalizer.

The radiation waiting area was coed, and we all wore the same type of gown. There were never more than three or four of us. Being creatures of habit, we usually arrived at the same time every day. Patients get this type of treatment Monday through Friday. I had thirty-six treatments. Once a week the doctor would check me out. Radiation burns the skin, and doctors keep an eye on the area being treated. Radiation also saps your strength, so they watch you closely to make sure you are staying well.

Three of us women, all breast cancer survivors, sat in a row. When the last of our little group was finished, several men would be bunched together. I think that this grouping helped the technicians to set up the machine. The people in this waiting room were more open than the chemo patients about what they were being treated for. Even making eye contact was hard in the chemo room. People were asleep or would turn away. In this room we became our own little support group. We would joke about how stylish our gowns were. As people finished their treatments, everyone would congratulate them and wish them the best with a handshake or a hug.

The next day there might be a new person in the time slot. All of us looked pretty much the same on our first day—wide-eyed and scared. People were polite and made small talk to help the novice adjust. Patients needed about a week to learn the routine and relax a little.

One man had his appointment after mine. I'm not sure what type of cancer he was being treated for, but he always came by himself. When his treatment was over, he would visit his son, who was in the hospital. His son had been partially paralyzed by a bullet. The man said he would help his son by moving his legs for him and massaging his arms. It is good to be reminded that there is always someone much worse off than we are. I thanked the Lord that my sons were well and safe.

A woman about my age always had her husband with her. I was interested to see how others coped with their illness. The patients who were believers seemed to sense each other, and we would witness a little about our faith and about how God was our strength. Some patients were bitter and angry and not much fun to be around.

The drive to my radiation appointment took twenty-five minutes, which was longer than my treatment took. Driving to my appointment was a big hurdle for me. We had not lived in the area long, and I had not become accustomed to the freeways. In North Carolina we were in a small town, and I was no longer comfortable in big-city traffic. John's health was bad and he couldn't drive, and I didn't want Jeff to have to take me every day. The only option left was to drive myself. I was telling one of the technicians about my fear of driving the freeway, and she mentioned a road that took only ten minutes longer. This route was perfect for me, so I took it. I prayed before I left the house, and I was blessed to get a time slot that was not during the heavy traffic hours. I felt as if God had worked everything out for me. He knew my weaknesses and my strengths.

The treatment took only ten minutes. The technicians would help me onto the table, line up my body, and match up the red grid lines with the little dots, reminding me not to move. Then they would leave the room and turn on the machine. It would move back and forth, and the next thing I knew the technicians would be in the room again, getting me up and scooting me out the door.

I had a friend send me some aloe gel packs that I would keep in the refrigerator and use on the radiation area to help with the burn. They felt cool and refreshing. The doctor also gave me samples of ointments and creams for the burn. I didn't seem to need them much. I had little burning. The doctor said I must have had healthy skin not to burn like other patients, but I gave God the credit because of all the prayer support I had. And if I had healthy skin, I gave God the credit for that.

The radiation depleted my energy. By the end of my treatments I wasn't doing much more than showering, going to the sessions, returning home, and taking a nap. I was so grateful that Jeff was with us to help John and do the shopping and the cooking.

There are occurrences in life that some would label coincidence but I would call God things. One of those God things happened to me on my next-to-last day of radiation. Jeff was getting ready to sell his truck. He had been talking about it and felt that the Lord was telling him to sell. We had not advertised the truck, which Jeff had inherited from my dad. My father had put stickers on the windows, including the Marine Corps symbol because of his service during World War II. Jeff had added a Christian decal.

I drove myself to treatment as usual, and as I was looking for a parking place a thought went through my head: *Ask the technicians if they know of anyone who wants to buy the truck.* I couldn't believe that this had occurred to me. As I was lying on the table for treatment, I asked the head technician if she knew of anyone who needed a gently used truck. In fact, one of the young men was looking for such a truck. Everything worked out beautifully, and he bought the truck from Jeff. The neat part is that he had been in the Marine Corps and was a believer, so the truck carried just the right stickers for him. I still see this technician from time to time when I go in for a routine checkup. He always gives me a big hug and tells me that the little truck is doing fine.

This was another miracle as far as I was concerned.

Chapter 8

It Is Finished!

By now I have had three procedures, two surgeries, six chemo treatments, thirty-six radiation treatments, and a year of healing. Then there were the countless blood tests, injections, scans, and doctor visits. All I want to do is return to normal—if I can remember what normal is. We had been in our house for only four weeks when I went for the first doctor visit. The whole experience seems like a dream, but when I look in the mirror I realize it was all true. From time to time I would take a picture of myself with my laptop. This seemed to help me mark the phases I was going through. None of it felt real.

Once I finished chemo, my hair slowly grew back. At first it was white all over. Some people call it chemo fuzz. I was told that when your hair grows back it may be different than what you had before it fell out. I was eager to find out what would happen with me. I had always thought that chemo patients got skinny. I put on weight! The nurses said that this happens to some patients. I decided that it was better to add weight than to be throwing up all the time and to become so thin that I was weak.

Recovering my normal strength took months. I was happy when I was able to do a chore like scrubbing the floor. I would have to divide the house and rest between mopping each section. John and Jeff were tired too. I'm sure they felt relief when I could start helping more often. It was so good to be home and not to need to visit a doctor's office every day. By the end of my treatments I was getting stressed about people coming at me with needles. These procedures were invasive, and I got tired of them and depressed about the treatments. I wanted my life back.

I was so glad to have my own hair back that I didn't care what it looked like. This was taken one Sunday when I came home from church.

It is now 2014 and most of what I have written about seems like it happened to someone else. My wigs and chemo caps are packed away, and using them is only a memory. After trying to keep my natural gray hair, I decided that I needed color in my life, so I returned to auburn. The natural curl has reappeared. I have scars from the surgeries, but I don't notice them anymore. I am still carrying the weight I put on. I have a slight numbness in the ends of my toes from the chemo treatments. Doctors had told me this might happen. By the grace of God and lots of prayers, the ordeal is over. Or is it?

A couple of months ago I had symptoms in my surgery area and in my right arm. I contacted Dr. Dao and he ordered tests starting that day. No one could figure out what caused the symptoms, and since then they have disappeared. All the tests gave me a good baseline in case I should need them in the future. Going through tests again was a little unnerving and challenged my faith. I realized that my life might be filled with tests now that I have had cancer. I needed to pull myself up and not slip into a depression.

One night I was lying in bed unable to sleep as I considered what might be happening to me. My thoughts turned to what I have written in this book about having faith. It is important that we praise God in all circumstances! I turned on my praise music and stuck both hands in the air. At first this was just a physical movement, but soon it became praise and worship. "I praise You, Lord," I said. "You are a great God who loves me and wants the best for me."

I thanked Him for the little things. "Thank You, Lord, for my bed, my lavender bedroom, the beautiful windows I can see out of, the sky, and the trees. Lord, I love You. I know You love me. I praise You for all that You have done for me. I praise You for everything You will do for me." I focused on Jesus. One of my favorite songs is "Turn Your Eyes upon Jesus" by Helen H. Lemmel. Here are the words of the chorus.

Turn your eyes upon Jesus. Look full in His wonderful face,
And the things of earth will grow strangely dim
In the light of His glory and grace.

I let the music continue to play and went to sleep. The next day was better, and in a couple of days the gloom of the unknown was gone.

As I write this, a friend has just been laid to rest. She and I were members of the same church, and while I was having my cancer treatments she was diagnosed with lung cancer. She had survived stage-four breast cancer several years before. This time she lost the battle against cancer. In the years that passed after her first cancer diagnosis, she found Jesus as her Savior. We would smile at each other from across the church sanctuary, and our eyes would meet as if to say, "I understand how you feel." I will miss her, but I am thankful that she is not suffering anymore. Thinking of her passing is a little scary. I could get cancer again. I tell myself that her breast cancer was much worse than mine and had spread throughout her body. I thank God mine was caught at an early stage. Someplace deep inside me, I feel that God somehow took care of the cancer and that it will never return.

I remember all of the things the doctors have told me to do and not to do. I try not to question the decisions I made during my treatments. When you are making choices like this, you weigh the percentages. How many patients did this and how many did that? How many lived to this age and how many lived to that age? There is so much to think about that a person could go crazy trying to take everything into consideration. Once you make these hard decisions, don't look back. Keep going with faith in God.

I hope and pray that no one else will learn that he or she has cancer, but that won't happen. I hope and pray that no one else will die from cancer, but that won't happen either, at least for now. We all need to pray that a cure for cancer will be found soon. Cancer doesn't take into consideration a person's age, race, or sex. It just strikes.

We can't always win the battle against cancer, but we can win the war if we have Jesus in our hearts. With Jesus as our Savior, we will go to heaven to be with Him, and in heaven there will be no illness or tears. "And I heard a loud voice from the throne saying, 'Now the dwelling of God is with men, and he will live with them. They will be his people, and God himself will be with them and be their God. He will wipe every tear from their eyes, There will be no more death or mourning or crying or pain, for the old order of things has passed away'" (Revelation 21:3–4).

Devotional

Lord, I Need Your Help

On many occasions I would think or say, "Lord, I need your help." Sometimes I would just think, *Lord*. I knew that He could hear me whether I spoke out loud or was silent. He knows our thoughts and our hearts' desires. A Scripture verse would sometimes pop into my head. These things lie deep in our minds, and God will bring them to the surface when we need them. He is always faithful to us.

Through others and through the work of the Holy Spirit, God wrote the Bible to guide our lives. It offers wisdom that has lasted throughout the ages. The Bible's truths are just as valid today as when they were first written.

I hope and pray that the following Bible verses and prayers will help you as Scripture and prayer helped me get through the hard times. Prayer draws us close to God. Scripture helps build our faith so it will remain strong and we can meet the challenges before us.

Please use the journal pages at the end of the devotional to record your journey.

Here are some possible subjects:

Did I hear God today?

What miracles are happening in my life?

What Scripture passage helped me today?

Was I able to bless someone else today?

How did I praise God today?

Anger

At some point you might become angry because of what you are enduring. God doesn't promise us a perfect life without hard situations, but He does promise to be with us during our trials. These Scripture verses will help you deal with anger.

"My dear brothers, take note of this: Everyone should be quick to listen, slow to speak and slow to become angry, for man's anger does not bring about the righteous life that God desires" (James 1:19–20).

"A fool gives full vent to his anger, but a wise man keeps himself under control" (Proverbs 29:11).

"A man's wisdom gives him patience; it is to his glory to overlook an offense" (Proverbs 19:11).

"Better a patient man than a warrior, a man who controls his temper than one who takes a city" (Proverbs 16:32).

"But now you must rid yourselves of all such things as these: anger, rage, malice, slander, and filthy language from your lips" (Colossians 3:8).

Prayer against anger:

Lord, please help me with this anger I am feeling. I lay my harsh emotions at the feet of Jesus and ask Him to remove these feelings from me. Help me to be at peace with the things that are causing my anger. I give You these things. (List the people or things that anger you.) I give You my feeling of injustice. Lord. I give thanks that You are with me and that You will rid me of this anger. In Jesus' name. Amen.

Faith

Don't put your faith in medications, treatments, or people. Put your faith in God, who will work through those medications, treatments, and people and use them to help you in ways that you would never imagine.

"Now faith is being sure of what we hope for and certain of what we do not see" (Hebrews 11:1).

"My message and my preaching were not with wise and persuasive words, but with a demonstration of the Spirit's power, so that your faith might not rest on men's wisdom, but on God's power" (1 Corinthians 2:4–5).

"We live by faith, not by sight" (2 Corinthians 5:7).

"Let us fix our eyes on Jesus, the author and perfecter of our faith, who for the joy set before him endured the cross, scorning its shame, and sat down at the right hand of the throne of God" (Hebrews 12:2).

"Consequently, faith comes from hearing the message, and the message is heard through the word of Christ" (Romans 10:17).

Prayer for faith:

Lord, Your Scriptures teach that we need faith only the size of a mustard seed. I pray that You will take what little faith I have and help it to grow. Help me to turn my concerns over to You. I know that You are in control of my life. In Jesus' name. Amen.

Fear

One night before one of my treatments I was scared and asked John and Jeff to pray with me. I didn't want to go to bed, because when I woke up I would be headed for a treatment. I don't know why fear took hold of me, but it did. As we prayed, Jeff got the sense that Jesus was holding His hand out to me to help me. Jesus wanted me to reach for Him. After asking the Lord to take my hand, I was able to relax and sleep.

"So do not fear, for I am with you; do not be dismayed, for I am your God. I will strengthen you and help you; I will uphold you with my righteous right hand" (Isaiah 41:10).

"For I am the Lord, your God, who takes hold of your right hand and says to you, Do not fear; I will help you" (Isaiah 41:13).

"You will not fear the terror of night, nor the arrow that flies by day, nor the pestilence that stalks in the darkness, nor the plague that destroys at midday" (Psalm 91:5).

"There is no fear in love. But perfect love drives out fear, because fear has to do with punishment" (1 John 5:18).

"But let all who take refuge in you be glad; let them ever sing for joy. Spread your protection over them, that those who love your name may rejoice in you" (Psalm 5:11).

"But Jesus came and touched them. 'Get up,' he said. 'Don't be afraid.' When they looked up, they saw no one except Jesus" (Matthew 17:7).

"Have I not commanded you? Be strong and courageous. Do not be terrified, do not be discouraged, for the Lord your God will be with you wherever you go" (Joshua 1:9).

Prayer against fear:

Lord, be with me today. I ask that You keep me free from all fear. I place the shield of faith in front of me to block all fear that might come at me. I pray that You fill me with the peace of Christ. Help me to be strong and courageous. In Jesus' name. Amen.

Trust

Children find it easy to trust. Life has not taught them hard lessons and turned them into skeptics. Jesus said, "Let the little children come to me, and do not hinder them, for the kingdom of God belongs to such as these. I tell you the truth, anyone who will not receive the kingdom of God like a little child will never enter it." The kingdom is in heaven and on earth. Heaven on earth is being close to God.

"Those who know your name trust in you, for you, Lord, have never forsaken those who seek you" (Psalm 9:10).

"To you, O Lord, I lift up my soul; in you I trust, O my God" (Psalm 25:1).

"The Lord is my strength and my shield; my heart trusts in him, and I am helped. My heart leaps for joy and I will give thanks to him in song" (Psalm 29:7).

"When I am afraid, I will trust in you. In God, whose word I praise, in God I trust; I will not be afraid" (Psalm 56:3–4).

"He who dwells in the shelter of the Most High will rest in the shadow of the Almighty. I will say of the Lord, 'He is my refuge and my fortress, my God in whom I trust'" (Psalm 91:1–2).

"He will have no fear of bad news; his heart is steadfast, trusting in the Lord. His heart is secure, he will have no fear; in the end he will look in triumph on his foes" (Psalm 112:7–8).

Prayer for trust:

Lord, I want to trust You. It is hard for me to do that. Please help me to understand that You love me more than anyone can and that You will protect and guide me. Help me to place all my cares and burdens in Your hands. You have the perfect plan for me. Help me to trust You.

Healing

Healing comes in many forms. As human beings, our first concern is usually our physical well-being. God cares most about our spiritual healing and our relationship with Him. He will often work on these things and leave the physical help to doctors. He will work through doctors and modern medical resources for our physical healing.

"Praise the Lord, O my soul, and forget not all his benefits—who forgives all your sins and heals all your diseases, who redeems your life from the pit and crowns you with love and compassion" (Psalm 103:2–4).

"The Lord will protect him and preserve his life; he will bless him in the land and not surrender him to the desire of his foes. The Lord will sustain him on his sickbed and restore him from his bed of illness" (Psalm 41:2–3).

"He heals the brokenhearted and binds up their wounds" (Psalm 147:3).

"Heal me, O Lord, and I will be healed; save me and I will be saved, for you are the one I praise" (Jeremiah 17:14).

"He will wipe every tear from their eyes. There will be no more death or mourning or crying or pain, for the old order of things has passed away" (Revelation 21:4).

"Therefore confess your sins to each other and pray for each other so that you may be healed. The prayer of a righteous man is powerful and effective" (James 5:16).

"He himself bore our sins in his body on the tree, so that we might die to sins and live for righteousness; by his wounds you have been healed" (1 Peter 2:24).

Prayer for healing:

Dear Lord, I ask that You heal my mind, my body, and my soul. Please help the medications do what they are meant to do. Cleanse my body of all unhealthy cells that might be developing. I pray that I will have no side effects from the medication. Please keep me healthy as I go through these treatments. In Jesus' name. Amen.

Hope

When we have hope we expect good things to happen. We are not positive they will happen, but we are waiting for a good outcome to our circumstances. We must remember that God wants only the best for us, and we should keep our hope in Him. He will never fail us. This doesn't mean that our road will be an easy one, but we will remain strong with hope.

"Joshua said to them, 'Do not be afraid; do not be discouraged. Be strong and courageous'" (Joshua 10:25).

"His pleasure is not in the strength of the horse, nor his delight in the legs of a man; the Lord delights in those who fear him, who put their hope in his unfailing love" (Psalm 147:10–11).

"Hope deferred makes the heart sick, but a longing fulfilled is a tree of life" (Proverbs 13:12).

"Therefore, since we have been justified through faith, we have peace with God through our Lord Jesus Christ, through whom we have gained access by faith into this grace in which we now stand. And we rejoice in the hope of the glory of God. Not only so, but we also rejoice in our sufferings, because we know that suffering produces perseverance, perseverance, character; and character, hope. And hope does not disappoint us, because God has poured out his love into our hearts by the Holy Spirit, whom he has given us" (Romans 5:1–7).

Prayer for hope:

O Father God, You are my hope and my strength. Help me to continue looking to You for help and keep me from falling into despair. Through You all things are possible. In Jesus' name. Amen.

Joy

Mary Poppins sang, "A spoonful of sugar helps the medicine goes down." It isn't easy to stay happy and in a good mood when you are going through something like cancer treatment, but it is important to do your best. Listening to uplifting music, hearing jokes or telling them, and keeping an attitude of gratitude can help. God is the one who can fill you with joy.

"May the God of hope fill you with all joy and peace as you trust in him, so that you may overflow with hope by the power of the Holy Spirit" (Romans 15:13).

"Nehemiah said, 'Go and enjoy choice food and sweet drinks, and send some to those who have nothing prepared. This day is sacred to our Lord. Do not grieve, for the joy of the Lord is your strength'" (Nehemiah 8:10).

"Then my head will be exalted above the enemies who surround me; at his tabernacle will I sacrifice with shouts of joy; I will sing and make music to the Lord" (Psalm 27:6).

"And the ransomed will walk there, and the ransomed of the Lord will return. They will enter Zion with singing; everlasting joy will crown their heads. Gladness and joy will overtake them, and sorrow and sighing will flee away" (Isaiah 35:10).

"So with you: Now is our time of grief, but I will see you again and you will rejoice, and no one will take away your joy" (John 16:22).

"Let us fix our eyes on Jesus, the author and perfecter of our faith, who for the joy set before him endured the cross, scorning its shame, and sat down at the right hand of the throne of God. Consider him who endured such opposition from sinful men, so that you will not grow weary and lose heart" (Hebrews 12:2).

Prayer for joy:

Lord, fill me with Your joy and chase away the darkness. Keep me in that safe, quiet place You have for me. Protect my thinking from the negative forces in the world. Help me to concentrate on You and on the joy in Your face when You look at me. In Jesus' name. Amen.

Strength

All of us have strengths and weaknesses. When we go through trials like cancer and its treatment, our weaknesses are magnified. Our strengths will take us only so far, and then we need a booster of some kind. The Lord is the best source of strength. He is tireless and is always there. He knows our needs before we do and is ready to help.

"I can do everything through him who gives me strength" (Philippians 4:13).

"He gives strength to the weary and increases the power of the weak. Even youths grow tired and weary, and young men stumble and fall; but those who hope in the Lord will renew their strength. They will soar on wings like eagles, they will run and not grow weary, they will walk and not be faint" (Isaiah 40:29–31).

"But you, O Lord, be not far off; O my Strength, come quickly to help me" (Psalm 22:19).

"The Lord is my strength and my shield; my heart trusts in him, and I am helped. My heart leaps for joy and I will give thanks to him in song. The Lord is the strength of his people, a fortress of salvation for his anointed one" (Psalm 28:7–8).

"The Sovereign Lord is my strength; he makes my feet like the feet of a deer, he enables me to go on the heights" (Habakkuk 3:19).

"I pray that out of his glorious riches he may strengthen you with power through his Spirit in your inner being, so that Christ may dwell in your hearts through faith" (Ephesians 3:16).

Prayer for strength:

Lord, I need You to strengthen me. Please strengthen me in every sense. Give me strength to do the physical things I need to do. Give me emotional strength to continue the treatment process. Give me spiritual strength so that I will not lose faith in You or in the people helping me. In Jesus' name. Amen.

Peace

Anyone facing uncertain times and undergoing new and invasive procedures will be afraid. It is all right to admit fear. I experienced different levels of fear, but at times I felt complete peace. I could feel the Holy Spirit minister to me and give me that peace. The way to achieve peace is through prayer and the Scriptures.

"I will lie down and sleep in peace, for you alone, O Lord, make me dwell in safety" (Psalm 4:8).

"You will keep in perfect peace him whose mind is steadfast, because he trusts in you. Trust in the Lord forever, for the Lord, the Lord, is the Rock eternal" (Isaiah 26:3–4).

"I have told you thee things, so that in me you may have peace. In this world you will have trouble. But take heart! I have overcome the world" (John 16:33).

"Do not be anxious about nothing, but in everything by prayer and petition, with thanksgiving, present your requests to God. And the peace of God, which transcends all understanding, will guard your hearts and your minds in Christ Jesus" (Philippians 4:6–7).

"But you, Bethlehem Ephrathah, though you are small among the clans of Judah, out of you will come for me one who will be ruler over Israel, whose origins are from of old, from ancient times. Therefore Israel will be abandoned until the time when she who is in labor gives birth and the rest of his brothers return to join the Israelites. He will stand and shepherd his flock in the strength of the Lord, in the majesty of the name of the Lord his God. And they will live securely, for then his greatness will reach to the ends of the earth. And he will be their peace" (Micah 5:2–5).

Prayer for peace:

Oh, Lord, I admit that there are things in my life right now that are causing me a lot of fear. I need Your peace to cover me. Please hide me under Your wing of safety and peace. Please bless me with peaceful sleep. Protect me from the side effects of the medications that keep me restless at night. In Jesus' name. Amen.

Thanksgiving

Going through treatments for cancer or any other illness isn't much fun, but it is better than the alternative. We are blessed that we live in a country with modern medicine and highly skilled doctors and nurses to help us get well.

"For everything God created is good, and nothing is to be rejected if it is received with thanksgiving, because it is consecrated by the word of God and prayer" (1 Timothy 4:4–5).

"Give thanks to the Lord, for he is good; his love endures forever" (1 Chronicles 16:34).

"I will give thanks to the Lord because of his righteousness and will sing praise to the name of the Lord Most High" (Psalm 7:17).

"Enter his gates with thanksgiving and his courts with praise; give thanks to him and praise his name" (Psalm 100:4).

"Give thanks to the Lord, for he is good; his love endures forever" (Psalm 106:1).

"Be joyful always; pray continually; give thanks in all circumstances, for this is God's will for you in Christ Jesus" (1 Thessalonians 5:16–18).

Prayer for thanksgiving:

Lord, I thank You for being with me during this time. I am thankful for all that You do for me. I thank You for the medications, doctors, and nurses helping me. I thank You for family and friends who are supporting me. Last but not least, I thank You for the things You are doing for me that I am unaware of. In Jesus' name. Amen.

Worry and Anxiety

There were times during my months of treatment when I could feel fear trying to overcome me. This usually happened at night when I couldn't sleep. To overcome the anxiety, I would turn to Scriptures, prayer, and praise music to give me peace.

"Consider the ravens: They do not sow or reap, they have no storeroom or barn; yet God feeds them, and how much more valuable you are than birds? Who of you by worrying can add a single hour to his life? Since you cannot do this very little thing, why do you worry about the rest?" (Luke 12:24–26).

"Peace I leave with you; my peace I give you. I do not give to you as the world gives. Do not let your hearts be troubled and do not be afraid" (John 14:27).

"Now may the Lord of peace himself give you peace at all times and in ever way. The Lord be with all of you" (2 Thessalonians 3:16).

"Cast your cares on the Lord and he will sustain you; he will never let the righteous fall" (Psalm 55:22).

"An anxious heart weighs a man down, but a kind word cheers him up" (Proverbs 12:25).

"Do not be anxious about anything, but in everything, by prayer and petition, with thanksgiving, present your request to God. And the peace of God, which transcends all understanding, will guard your hearts and your minds in Christ Jesus" (Philippians 4:6–7).

"Trust in the Lord with all your heart and lean not on your own understanding; in all your ways acknowledge him, and he will make your paths straight" (Proverbs 3:5).

"Cast all your anxiety on him because he cares for you" (1 Peter 5:7).

Prayer for anxiety and worry:

Heavenly Father, I know that You are watching over me and all that is going on around me. I give You all my concerns and worries. (Name the things that are bothering you.) I understand that You know what is best for me. You are in control. In Jesus' name. Amen.

Salvation

The one thing that we know for sure about God's will is that He doesn't want anyone to go to hell but wants all of us to be with Him in heaven. When God created humans, He gave us free will. Thus we can decide whether to give our lives to God. If we choose salvation, won by Christ's death on the cross for us, we go to heaven. If we choose not to accept Christ, we go to hell. Either destination is for all eternity. We do not get to heaven by being nice to others or by leading a clean life or because our parents went to church. We gain salvation only by asking God to forgive our sins and by acknowledging that Christ died, was buried, and rose from the grave for us. The four paragraphs below will help you to understand.

1. "For God so loved the world that He gave His one and only Son, that whoever believes in Him shall not perish but have eternal life" (John 3:16). God loves us more than we will ever know.
2. "There is no difference, for all have sinned and fall short of the glory of God, and are justified freely by his grace through the redemption that came by Christ Jesus" (Romans 3:23). Because of Adam and Eve and their sin, we are all born into sin. We are all sinners.
3. "But God demonstrates His own love for us in this: while we were still sinners, Christ died for us" (Romans 5:8). Christ is the bridge between us and God. We can't reach God without Him.
4. "For it is by grace you have been saved, through faith—and that not of yourselves, it is the gift of God—not as a result of works, so that no one can

boast" (Ephesians 2:8–9). All of us must understand in our hearts that Jesus died for us and ask Him to come into our hearts and rule our lives.

Prayer to receive Christ as your Savior:

Jesus, I know that You love me and died for me. I am sorry that I have sinned against You. Please forgive me. I want You to live in my heart forever. Amen.

The Lord's Prayer

Jesus gave us the Lord's Prayer because it includes everything that we need to know how to pray. In this prayer, we praise God, ask Him to take care of us, beg forgiveness for our sins, forgive others, seek protection, and ask that God's will rule here on earth. This is what I would pray when I didn't know what to pray for.

"One day Jesus was praying in a certain place. When he finished, one of his disciples said to him, 'Lord, teach us to pray, just as John taught his disciples.' He said to them, 'When you pray, say: Father, hollowed by your name, your kingdom come. Give us each day our daily bread. Forgive us our sins, for we also forgive everyone who sins against us. And lead us not into temptation'" (Luke 11:1–2).

"This, then, is how you should pray: 'Our Father in heaven, hallowed be our name, your kingdom come, your will be done on earth as it is in heaven. Give us today our daily bread. Forgive us our debts, as we also have forgiven our debtors. And lead us not into temptation, but deliver us from the evil one" (Matthew 6:9–13).

This is the traditional Lord's Prayer that we use today:

Our Father, which are in heaven, hallowed by thy name. Thy kingdom come. Thy will be done in earth, as it is in heaven. Give us this day our daily bread. And forgive us our trespasses, as we forgive them that trespass against us. And lead us not into temptation, but deliver us from evil. For thine is the kingdom, the power, and the glory, for ever and ever. Amen.

Psalm 23

A psalm of David

The Lord is my shepherd, I shall not be in want. He makes me lie down in green pastures, he leads me beside quiet waters, he restores my soul. He guides me in paths of righteousness for his name's sake. Even though I walk through the valley of the shadow of death, I will fear no evil, for you are with me; your rod and your staff, they comfort me. You prepare a table before me in the presence of my enemies. You anoint my head with oil; my cup overflows. Surely goodness and love will follow me all the days of my life, and I will dwell in the house of the Lord forever.

Journal

Journal

Journal

Journal

Journal

Journal

Journal

www.ingramcontent.com/pod-product-compliance
Ingram Content Group UK Ltd.
Pitfield, Milton Keynes, MK11 3LW, UK
UKHW040019200726
13854UKWH00001B/273

9 781490 854403